THE CHRISTIAN ARMORY

EQUIPPING THE BELIEVER

MOODY
Chicago

THE CHRISTIAN'S ARMORY
EQUIPPING THE BELIEVER

© Copyright 1992
by Schwalb Creative Communications Inc.
P.O. Box 291206
Nashville, TN 37229

Printed in the United States of America

Published by:
Moody Press
Chicago

THE CHRISTIAN ARMORY

EQUIPPING THE BELIEVER

BE STRONG IN THE LORD,
AND IN THE POWER OF HIS MIGHT.
PUT ON THE WHOLE ARMOR OF GOD,
THAT YOU MAY BE ABLE TO STAND
AGAINST THE CLEVER STRATEGIES
OF THE DESTROYER.
FOR WE WRESTLE NOT AGAINST
FLESH AND BLOOD,
BUT AGAINST PRINCIPALITIES,
AGAINST POWERS,
AGAINST THE RULERS OF DARKNESS
OF THIS WORLD,
AGAINST SPIRITUAL WICKEDNESS
IN HIGH PLACES.
WHEREFORE TAKE UNTO YOU
THE WHOLE ARMOR OF GOD,
THAT YOU MAY BE ABLE
TO WITHSTAND
IN THE EVIL DAY,
AND HAVING DONE ALL,
TO STAND.

Ephesians 6:14

*Stand
and gird up
your loins
with
truth.*

Remains of a Roman infantryman's grave marker showing twin belts
and apron, 1st century A. D., Rheinisches Landemuseum, Bonn, Germany.

The Girdle of Truth

To gird up one's loins means to get ready to do something strenuous. It is similar to what a weightlifter does in preparing to hoist a huge weight. Paul, in his letter to the Ephesians, speaks about the strenuous task believers face in overcoming the world and refers to the preparations of a soldier—a Roman legionary.

In preparing for battle, soldiers removed any cumbersome clothing, but left on a loose-fitting woolen tunic which was hitched up at the waist to allow freedom of movement. Over this they would place their breastplates or coats of mail and bind them on with a belt-like girdle (*cingulum*) that would keep them in place, help take their weight off the shoulders, and offer protection to the lower abdomen. In the front, hanging from the belt, was an apron of leather strips decorated with medallions and bits of metal. They offered added protection, and, some say a psychological advantage too. As troops marched into battle, the clinking of the medallions and the resultant flashes of light from their movement intimidated their opponents.

A reconstructed belt based on fittings found in Illyricum.

6

For the LORD has girded us with strength to battle by the word of truth, by the power of God, by the armor of righteousness on the right hand and on the left.

Wherefore seeing we also are surrounded with so great a cloud of witnesses, let us lay aside every weight —the sin which does so easily beset us: laying aside all malice, and all guile, and hypocrisies, and envies, and all evil talk. We as newborn babes desire the sincere milk of the word, that we may grow thereby: if so we have tasted that the Lord is gracious, how sweet are His words to our taste! yes, sweeter than honey in our mouth!

Through the Lord's precepts we get understanding: therefore we hate every false way. The Lord is good; His mercy is everlasting; and His truth endures to all generations.

The Lord is near, and all His commandments are truth. For the word of the Lord is right; and all His works are done in truth.

Therefore, lead us in Your truth, and teach us. Do not withhold Your tender

mercies from us, O Lord: let Your lov-
ingkindness and Your truth continually
preserve us.

Behold, You desire truth in the
inward parts: and in the hidden part
You shall make us to know wisdom.
Your word have we hid in our hearts
that we might not sin against You. For
You are great, and do wondrous things:
You are God alone. Teach us Your way,
O Lord; we will walk in Your truth:
unite our hearts to fear Your name.

If we lack wisdom, let us ask of God,
who gives to all people liberally, and
chides not; and it shall be given to us.
But let us ask in faith, not wavering.
For they that waver are like a wave of
the sea driven with the wind and tossed
about. For those people should not
think that they shall receive anything
of the Lord.

Wherefore lay apart all filthiness
and excessive behavior, and meekly
receive the engrafted word, which is
able to save our souls.

We should be doers of the word, and
not hearers only. Let us not love in
word; but in deed and in truth. And

hereby we know that we are of the truth, and shall assure our hearts before Him.

Wherefore gird up the loins of your mind, be sober, and hope to the end for the grace that is to be brought to you at the revelation of Jesus Christ; as obedient children, not fashioning yourselves according to the former lusts in your ignorance: but as He who has called you is holy, so we should be holy in every part of our life; because it is written, "For I am the Lord your God: you shall therefore sanctify yourselves, and you shall be holy; for I am holy." Even Jesus asked His Father to sanctify us through His truth: His word is truth and we shall know the truth and the truth shall make us free. Forasmuch as we know that we were not redeemed with corruptible things, as silver and gold, but with the precious blood of Christ, as of a lamb without blemish and without spot: who truly was foreordained before the foundation of the world, but was revealed in these last times for us; we believe that God raised Him up from the dead, and gave Him glory; that our faith and hope might be in God. We have purified our souls in obeying the truth through the Spirit with unfeigned love toward others; we love one another with a pure heart fervently: being born again, not of corruptible seed, but of incorruptible, by the word of God, which lives and abides for ever. For all flesh is as grass, and all the glory of man as the flower of grass. The grass withers, and its flower falls away: but the word of the Lord endures for ever.

And this is the word which is preached to us. If we love Jesus, we will keep Jesus' words: and His Father will love us, and They will come to us and make Their abode with us. Even the Spirit of truth; which proceeds from the Father, He shall testify of Jesus: He shall teach us all things, and bring all things to our remembrance, whatsoever Jesus has said. He shall glorify Jesus: for He shall receive of Him, and show it to us.

Therefore, You, Lord, have girded us with strength unto the battle: You have subdued under us those that rose up against us. No evil shall befall us; neither shall any plague come close to us. Though we walk in the middle of trouble, You will revive us: You will stretch forth Your hand against the wrath of our enemies, and Your right hand shall save us. You, Lord, will perfect that which concerns us: Your mercy, O Lord, endures for ever.

You have turned our mourning into dancing: You have taken off our sackcloth, and girded us with gladness. O Lord our God, we will give thanks to You for ever.

REFERENCES:

Ps. 18:39	1 John 3:18–19
2 Cor. 6:7	1 Pet. 1:13–16
Heb. 12:1	Lev. 11:44
1 Pet. 2:1–3	John 17:17
Ps. 119:103–4	John 8: 32
Ps. 100:5	1 Pet. 1:18–25
Ps. 119:151	John 14:23
Ps. 33:4	John 15:26
Ps. 25:5	John 14:26
Ps. 40:11	John 16:14
Ps. 51:6	Ps. 18:39
Ps. 119:11	Ps. 91:10
Ps. 86:10–11	Ps. 138:7–8
James 1:5–7; 21–22	Ps. 30:11–12

*Put on
the
breastplate
of
righteousness.*

Centurion Marcus Favonias Facilis' grave marker shows him wearing a metal cuirass with decorative shoulder-pieces. In his right hand is a vine stick *(vitis)*, a symbol of his rank, 49 A.D., Colchester Museum, Colchester, Great Britain.

The Breastplate of Righteousness

The English Bible translates a number of different words as breastplate. In 1 Thessalonians 5:8 the word translated refers to a coat of mail made up of front and back pieces. Paul uses it to symbolize that faith and love are joined together to become a garment of protection.

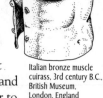

Italian bronze muscle cuirass, 3rd century B.C., British Museum, London, England

Paul, in his letter to the Ephesians, refers to Isaiah 59:17 and has another word in mind. The word Paul used was the word *thōrax*—the word for cuirass— chest armor made up of two sculpted brass plates hammered to fit their owners with anatomical perfection. They were worn as a symbol of rank by centurions and other leaders in the Roman legion. Paul's use of the word *thōrax* tells us that as believers, our righteousness should conform to every part of our person and that this righteousness helps others to see that they should follow our example in faith and practice.

The night is far spent, the day is at hand: let us therefore cast off the works of darkness, and let us put on the armor of light. Let us walk honestly, as in the day; not in rioting and drunkenness, not in debauchery and immorality, not in strife and envying. But let us put on the Lord Jesus Christ, and make no provision for the flesh, nor its lusts. But let us, who are of the day, be sober, and put on the breastplate of faith. For God has not appointed us to wrath, but to obtain salvation by our Lord Jesus Christ.

From this day forward there are laid up for us crowns of righteousness, which the Lord, the righteous judge, shall give us at that day: and not to us only, but also to all them that love His appearing.

Therefore, we put on righteousness, and it clothed us: our judgment was as a robe and a diadem. We are the eyes to the blind, and feet to the lame. We are a father to the poor: and the cause which we knew not we searched out. And we broke the jaws of the wicked, and plucked the spoil out of his teeth.

For God too puts on righteousness as a breastplate, and an helmet of salvation upon His head; and He puts on the garments of vengeance for clothing, and is clad with zeal as a cloak. His righteousness is an everlasting righteousness, and His law is the truth.

Trouble and anguish have taken hold on us: yet God's commandments are our delight. The righteousness of God's testimonies is everlasting: therefore, O Lord, give us understanding, and we shall live. For blessed are they that keep judgment, and they that do righteousness at all times. In righteousness shall we be established; for we shall not fear: and from terror, for it shall not come near us. Behold the enemy shall surely gather together, but not by us: whosoever shall gather together against us shall fall for God's sake. Behold God has created the smith that blows the coals in the fire, and that brings forth an instrument for His work; and He has created the waster to destroy the enemy. No weapon that is formed against us shall prosper; and every tongue that shall rise against us in judgment God shall condemn. This is the heritage of the servants of the Lord. "Their righteousness is of me," says the Lord.

Therefore in You, O Lord, do we put our trust: let us never be put to confusion. Behold, we have longed after Your precepts: bring to life Your righteousness in us. Deliver us in Your righteousness, and cause us to escape the evil one. Incline Your ear unto us, and save us. Be our strong habitation, where we may continually resort for You have given us commandments to save us; for You are our rock and our fortress.

Therefore we will seek first the kingdom of God, and His righteousness; even the righteousness of God which is by faith of Jesus Christ unto all and upon all that believe. For therein is the righteousness of God revealed from faith to faith: as it is written, "The just shall live by faith." For what does the Scripture say? "Abraham believed God, and his faith was counted for righteousness." Now to us that believe on Him that justified the ungodly, our faith is counted for righteousness. For if we shall confess with our mouth the Lord Jesus, and shall believe in our hearts that God has raised Him from the dead, we shall be saved. For with the heart man believes to righteousness; and with the mouth confession is made unto salvation.

Then shall we understand righteousness, and judgment, and equity; yes, every good path we should travel. When wisdom enters into our hearts: knowledge is pleasant to our souls. Discretion shall preserve us: understanding shall keep us. If we make sure to do all these commandments before the Lord our God, as He has commanded us, it shall be our righteousness.

Herein is a lesson for us that we should not walk as the worldly-minded walk, in the vanity of their mind, having their understanding darkened, being alienated from the life of God through the ignorance that is in them, because of the blindness of their heart: who being past feeling have given themselves over to lustful desires, to greedily work all uncleanness. But we have not so learned Christ; if so be that we have heard Him, and have been taught by Him, as the truth is in Jesus: that we put off concerning the former life the old man, which is corrupt according to the deceitful lusts; and being renewed in the spirit of our minds, put on the new man, which after God is created in righteousness and true holiness. Wherefore putting away lying, we speak the truth with our neighbor: for we are members one of another. We will work out our anger, and sin not: we will not let not the sun set being filled with wrath: neither will we give place to the devil. Let him that stole steal no more: but rather let him labor, working with his hands the thing which is good, so that he may have in order to give to the needy. Let no corrupt communication proceed out of our mouth, but rather that which helps to edify, that it may minister grace to those that hear.

Lord, who shall abide in Your tabernacle? Who shall dwell in Your holy hill? He that walks uprightly, and works righteousness, and speaks the truth in his heart. He that does not backbite, do evil, or seek to stir up trouble with his neighbor. Nor he that takes advantage of the innocent or those in need.

We should not be unequally yoked together with unbelievers: for what fellowship does righteousness have with unrighteousness? And what communion has light with darkness? We should flee youthful lusts: and rather follow righteousness, faith, charity, peace, with them that call on the Lord out of a pure heart.

Remember it is in God's eyes that a vile person is condemned; but God honors them that fear Him. He that swears, swears to his own hurt. Therefore do not grieve the Holy Spirit of God, whereby we are sealed to the day of redemption. Let all bitterness, and wrath, and anger, and clamor, and evil speaking be put away from us, with all malice: for the wrath of man does not work the righteousness of God. Treasures of wickedness profit nothing: but righteousness delivers from death.

Furthermore we should not yield our bodies as instruments of unrighteousness to sin: but rather we should yield ourselves to God, as those who are alive from the dead, and our bodies as instruments of righteousness unto God.

The way of righteousness is life; in its pathway there is no death. He that follows after righteousness and mercy will find life, righteousness, and honor. We are in Christ Jesus, whom God has made to us wisdom, and righteousness, and sanctification, and redemption.

Therefore, as people of God, we will flee evil things and follow after righteousness, godliness, faith, love, patience, meekness. We will fight the good fight of faith, laying hold on eternal life, to which we have been called. We will be sure to make a good profession before many witnesses. And we will be kind to others, tenderhearted, forgiving each other, even as God for Christ's sake has forgiven us.

O Lord, lead us in Your righteousness because the evil one would lead us astray; make Your way clear to us. And righteousness and faithfulness shall be the girdle of our loins, and our assurance for ever.

REFERENCES

Rom. 13:12–14
1 Thess. 5:8–9
2 Tim. 4:8
Job 29:14–17
Isa. 59:17
Ps. 119:142–44
Ps. 106:3
Isa. 59:14-17
Ps. 71:1
Ps. 119:40
Ps. 71:2–3
Matt. 6:33
Rom. 3:22
Rom. 1:17
Rom. 4:3, 5
Rom. 10:9–10
Prov. 2:9–11
Deut. 6:25

Eph. 4:17–29
Ps. 15:1–3, 5
2 Cor. 6:14
2 Tim. 2:22
Ps. 15:4
Eph. 4:30–31
James 1:20
Prov. 10:2
Rom. 6:13
Prov. 12:28
Prov. 21:21
1 Cor. 1:30
1 Tim. 6:11–12
Eph. 4:32
Ps. 5:8
Isa. 11:5
Isa. 32:17

Ephesians 6:15

Cover
your feet
with the
preparation
of the
gospel
of peace.

Common Roman military boot *(caliga)*.

Covered with the Preparation of the Gospel of Peace

Roman soldiers wore hobbed sandals (*caliga*) on their feet. These sandals by their very nature could not be slipped on and off like today's sandals, as they each were made from one piece of leather, stitched up the back and laced up the front. Before battle or reporting for duty, the soldier had a whole ritual of preparation, from lacing on his sandals to anointing his shield.

On the bottom of the sandals was stitched a one-half inch thick sole made up of many layers of leather and studded with iron hob nails. The hobnails provided firm traction in the muck and mire of the battlefield, and the thick leather sole offered protection against sharp spikes (*caltrap*) that were sprinkled on the ground by the enemy.

A caltrap.

The layout of the *caliga* with iron studded sole.

Though an army should encamp against us, our hearts shall not fear: though war should rise against us, we will not be troubled. For in the world we will have tribulation; but we can be of good cheer for Jesus has overcome the world. He will keep us from the snares which the enemy has laid for us, and from the traps of the workers of iniquity. Rather the wicked fall into their own nets, while we escape. Even though the wicked have dug a pit to take us, and hidden snares, we will not depart from God's precepts, because He has brought us up out of a horrible pit, out of the miry clay, and set our feet upon a rock and established our goings. Thus when the wicked, even our enemies and foes, come upon us to eat up our flesh, they will stumble and fall. For the way of the wicked is as darkness: they do not know at what they stumble.

In this we can be confident; we will call upon God, and the Lord shall save us. Evening, and morning, and at noon, we will pray, and cry aloud: and He shall hear our voice.

He has delivered our souls in peace

from the battle that was against us: for there are many with us. For He has given His angels charge over us, to keep us in all His ways. They shall bear us up in their hands, lest we dash our feet against a stone.

Therefore we shall tread upon the lion and adder: the young lion and the dragon we will trample under our feet. The adversaries of the Lord shall be broken to pieces, and the God of peace shall bruise Satan under our feet. God will keep the feet of His saints, and the wicked shall be silent in darkness.

Even though we walk through the valley of the shadow of death, we will fear no evil: for God is with us.

Our souls can return to rest for the Lord has bountifully dealt with us. He has delivered our souls from death, our eyes from tears, and our feet from falling. We will walk before the Lord in the land of the living. The Lord will give strength to His people; the Lord will bless His people with peace.

His light and truth will lead us; they will bring us to His holy hill, and to His tabernacles. For the Lord's paths are mercy and truth for those who keep His covenant and His testimonies. His word will keep us from the paths of the destroyer. He will support us as we travel His paths, so that our footsteps will not slip. God Himself will make our way perfect. He will make our feet like hinds' feet and set us upon high places. He will enlarge our steps under us so that our feet will not slip.

We will trust in God, because we have heard the word of truth, the gospel of our salvation: in whom also after that we believed, we were sealed with the Holy Spirit as promised.

Therefore we will make all our needs known through prayer and supplication with thanksgiving. And the peace of God, which passes all understanding, will keep our hearts and minds through Christ Jesus.

Therefore we will think on whatsoever things are true, whatsoever things are honest, whatsoever things are just, whatsoever things are pure, whatsoever things are lovely, and whatsoever things are of good report. If there be any virtue, and if there be any praise, we will think on those things. And will do those things which Jesus did. We will put on mercy, kindness, humility, meekness, patience; and help keep each other from quarreling by forgiving one another even as Christ has forgiven us. And over all these things we will put on love, which binds them together perfectly.

We will warn them that are unruly, comfort the faint-hearted, support the weak, be patient toward all. We will see that no one renders evil for evil to any person; but ever follow that which is good with all.

We will rejoice evermore. Pray without ceasing. In every thing give thanks: for this is the will of God in Christ Jesus concerning us.

We will not quench the Spirit, nor despise prophesyings but rather prove all things and hold fast that which is good.

We will abstain from all appearance of evil.

And doing so, the very God of peace will sanctify us wholly; and our whole spirit and soul and body will be preserved blameless unto the coming of our Lord Jesus Christ. Because faithful is He that called us, who also will do it.

And it is good advice to mark them which cause divisions and offenses contrary to the doctrine which we have learned, and avoid them. For they that are such serve not our Lord Jesus Christ, but their own belly, and by good words and fair speeches deceive the hearts of the simple. God is not the author of confusion, but of peace.

Rather we will let the peace of God rule in our hearts, which will make us one body; and we will be thankful. We will let the word of Christ dwell in us richly, and we will teach and admonish one another with psalms and hymns and spiritual songs, singing with grace in our hearts to the Lord. And whatsoever we do, whether it be in word or deed, we will do all in the name of the Lord Jesus.

For Jesus is our peace. He came and preached peace to us which were afar off, and to them that were near. For through Him we both have access by one Spirit unto the Father. Now therefore we are no more strangers and foreigners, but fellow citizens with the saints, and of the household of God.

We are built upon the foundation of the apostles and prophets, Jesus Christ Himself being the chief cornerstone; in whom all the building is perfectly joined together and grows to become a holy temple in the Lord: in whom we are together built for an habitation for God through the Spirit.

For the kingdom of God is righteousness, and peace, and joy in the Holy Ghost. And the peace of God, which surpasses all understanding, will guard our hearts and minds through Christ Jesus.

REFERENCES:

Ps. 28:3
John 16:33
Ps. 141:9–10
Isa. 18:22
Ps. 119:110
Ps. 40:2
Ps. 282
Prov. 4:19
Ps. 27:3
Ps. 55:16–17
Ps. 91:11–13
1 Sam. 2:10
Rom. 6:20
1 Sam. 2:9
Ps. 23:4
Ps. 116:7–9

Ps. 29:11
Ps. 43:3
Ps. 25:10
Ps. 17:4–5
Ps. 18:32–33, 36
Eph. 1:13
Phil. 4:6–9
Col. 3:12–14
1 Thess. 5:14–24
Rom. 16:17–18
1 Cor. 14:33
Col. 3:15-17
Eph. 2:14, 17–22
Rom. 14:17
Phil. 4:7

Ephesians 6:16

Take the shield of faith, with which you will be able to quench all the fiery darts of the wicked.

Bas relief of a legionary in battle, left shoulder in shield, right hand ready to thrust with the sword. 1st century A.D. Romisch Germanisches Zentral-museum, Mainz, Germany.

The Shield of Faith

When Paul speaks of the shield
in Ephesians he uses the Greek
word (*thureon*) derived from the
root *thyra*, or door, which most
likely refers to the size and shape
of the shield (*scutum*) carried by
Roman legionaries—approxi-
mately four feet long by two-
and-one-half feet wide and
three inches thick. Built upon

The *scutum.*

either an iron frame or a laminated wood
base, this shield was covered with layers of
leather. The leather covering was soaked
in water prior to battle to make it flame
resistant and to make it slippery to help
deflect blows. The shield also was curved
to help deflect stones, pikes, and other
missiles. In the center of the shield was a
convex iron plate—a boss—that protected
the shield's hand hold.

The Roman infantry was famous for its
testudo, or tortoise formation, in which
these massive shields were overlapped to
make an impenetrable covering that protected its troops from flying
missiles. It was claimed
to be strong enough to
withstand being driven
over by a cart.

Testudo formation.

God has also given you the shield of His salvation: and His right hand has held you up, and His gentleness has made you great.

Behold, O God, our shield. He shall cover us with His feathers, and under His wings shall we trust: His truth shall be our shield and buckler. Every word of God is pure: He is a shield unto them that put their trust in Him.

Beloved, think it not strange concerning the fiery trial which is to try you, as though some strange thing happened to you: for the wicked bend their bow, they make ready their arrow upon the string, that they may in ambush shoot at the upright in heart. But rejoice, inasmuch as you are partakers of Christ's sufferings; that, when His glory shall be revealed, you may be glad also with exceeding joy. What more should be said? For there is not enough time to tell of Gideon, and of Barak, and of Samson, and of Jephthah; of David also and Samuel, and of the prophets: who through faith subdued kingdoms, wrought righteousness, obtained promises, stopped the mouths of lions, quenched the violence of fire, escaped the edge of the sword, grew valiant in fight, turned to flight the armies of the aliens.

Therefore, we shall not be afraid for the terror by night; nor for the arrow that flies by day; nor for the pestilence that walks in darkness; nor for the destruction that wastes at noonday. A thousand shall fall at our side, and ten thousand at our right hand; but it shall not come near us. Let not our heart be troubled: we believe in God, believe also in Jesus. For God is a shield for us, He is our glory and will lift up our heads.

The time is fulfilled, and the kingdom of God is at hand: repent and believe the gospel.

Now faith is the substance of things hoped for, the evidence of things not seen.

Watch, stand fast in the faith, be strong like men. Be sober, be vigilant; because your adversary the devil walks around as a roaring lion, seeking whom he may devour: the devil is come down to you, having great wrath, because he knows that he hath but a short time. Resist the devil, steadfast in the faith…. confirming the souls of the disciples, and exhorting them to continue in the faith, and that we must through much tribulation enter into the kingdom of God. Tell them that the Lord will bless the righteous; with favor will He encircle them as with a shield.

This is the work of God, that we believe on Him whom He has sent. The fruit of the Spirit is love, joy, peace, longsuffering, gentleness, goodness, faith.

Therefore, our soul waits for the Lord: He is our help and our shield. Our heart shall rejoice in Him, because we have trusted in His holy name, that through His name whosoever believes in Him shall receive remission of sins.

Believe on the Lord Jesus Christ, and you shall be saved, and your house. For God so loved the world, that He gave His only begotten Son, that whosoever believes in Him should not perish, but have everlasting life. He that believes and is baptized shall be saved; but he that doesn't believe shall be damned.

He that believes on Him is not condemned: but he that does not believe is
condemned already. But as many as
received Him to them gave He power
to become sons of God, even to them
that believe on His name. In whom we
have boldness and access with confi-
dence by the faith of Him. For that He
would grant you, according to the riches of his glory, to be strengthened with
might by His Spirit in the inner person;
that Christ may dwell in our hearts by
faith; that we being rooted and grounded in love may be able to comprehend
with all saints what is the breadth, and
length, and depth, and height, and to
know the love of Christ, which passes
knowledge, that we might be filled with
all the fullness of God. God is our
strength and our shield; our hearts trust
in Him and we are helped.

Let our entire life complement the
gospel of Christ: that we stand fast in
one spirit, with one mind striving
together for the faith of the gospel and
in nothing terrified by our adversaries:
which is to them evidence of perdition,
but to us salvation, and that of God.

This will open the eyes of others, and turn them from darkness to light, and from the power of Satan to God, that they may receive forgiveness of sins and inheritance among them which are sanctified by faith that is in Jesus. Therefore being justified by faith, we have peace with God through our Lord Jesus Christ: by whom also we have access by faith into this grace wherein we stand, and rejoice in hope of the glory of God.

Jesus is the resurrection, and the life: they that believe in Him, though they were dead, yet shall they live: and whosoever lives and believes in Jesus shall never die.

Whatsoever we shall ask in prayer, believing, we shall receive. If we have faith as a grain of mustard seed, we shall say to a mountain, "Move over there," and it shall move, and nothing shall be impossible to you.

We need faith like that of Abraham, who hoped against hope that he would father many nations as had been promised him by God even though he and his wife Sarah were well past childbearing age. He did not waver at the promise of God through unbelief, but was strong in faith, giving glory to God and being fully persuaded that, what God had promised, He was able to perform.

It pleased the Father that in Jesus should all fullness dwell; and, having made peace through the blood of Christ's cross, by Jesus to reconcile all things to Himself. And we that were sometime alienated and enemies in our mind by wicked works, yet now Jesus reconciled in the body of His flesh through death, to present us holy and unblamable and unreprovable in the Father's sight: if we continue in the faith grounded and settled, and are not moved away from the hope of the gospel.

We know whom we have believed and therefore we are persuaded that He is able to keep that which has been committed to Him. We shall never perish, neither shall any man pluck us out of the hand of God.

Therefore we put our trust under the shadow of God's wings. He will not let the foot of pride come against us, and will not let the hand of the wicked remove us; for His faithfulness reaches to the clouds. His faithfulness is to all generations. His covenant He will not break, nor alter the thing that is gone out of His lips.

Who in heaven can be compared to You? O Lord God of hosts, who is a strong Lord like You? Your faithfulness surrounds You. You will build up Your mercy forever. You will establish Your faithfulness in the very heavens. Great is Your faithfulness, O Lord our shield.

You, Lord, will be a refuge for us who are oppressed, You will be a refuge in times of trouble. We who know You will put our complete trust in you: for You, Lord, have never forsaken them that seek You.

This is the victory that overcomes the world, even our faith. Who is he that overcomes the world, but he that believes that Jesus is the Son of God. Thanks be to God, who gives us the victory through our Lord Jesus Christ.

REFERENCES:

Ps. 19:35
Ps. 89:9
Ps. 91:4
Prov. 30:5
1 Pet. 4:12
Ps. 11:2
1 Pet. 4:13
Heb. 11:32–34
Ps. 91:4
John 14:1
Ps. 3:3
Mark 1:15
Heb. 11:1
1 Cor. 16:13
1 Pet. 5:8
Rev. 12:12
1 Pet. 5:9
Acts 14:22
Ps. 5:12
John 6:29
Gal. 5:22
Ps. 33:20
Acts 10:43
Acts 16:31
John 3:16
Mark 16:16

John 3:18
John 1:12
Eph. 3:12, 16–19
Ps. 28:7
Phil. 1:27
Acts 26:18
Rom. 5:1–2
John 11:25–26
Matt. 21:22
Matt. 17:20
Rom. 4:18–22
Col. 1:19–23
2 Tim. 1:12
John 10:28–29
Ps. 36:7, 11
Ps. 36:5
Ps. 119:90
Ps. 89:34
Ps. 89:6, 8
Ps. 89:2
Lam. 3:23
Ps. 59:11
Ps. 9:9
1 John 5:4–5
1 Cor. 15:57

Heartily accept the helmet of salvation.

The centurion's staff (vitis), helmet with transverse crest, and leg greaves from the grave marker of T. Calidius Serverus.
Kunsthistorisches Museum, Vienna, Austria.

The Helmet of Salvation

Forged from a single piece of metal, the Roman helmet featured a unique shape that protected its wearer from blows to the back of the neck and the upper shoulders as well as to the top of the head. Cheek pieces were added to protect the face, and later, iron cross-braces were riveted onto the top to further strengthen the helmet.

For comfort, the interior of the helmet was padded and a clever system of straps threaded through rings on the neck guard, crossed at the throat, threaded through more rings inside the cheek pieces, and tied off under the chin. These straps made it impossible for the helmet to come off during battle.

Reinforced infantry helmet, c. 100 to 200 A.D.
Israel Museum, Jerusalem, Israel.

O God the Lord, the strength of my salvation, You have covered our heads in the day of battle. We will greatly rejoice in the Lord, our souls shall be joyful in our God; for He has clothed us with the garments of salvation, He has covered us with the robe of righteousness. Neither is there salvation in any other: for there is no other name under heaven given among men, whereby we must be saved. If we confess with our mouths the Lord Jesus, and shall believe in our hearts that God has raised Him from the dead, we will be saved.

Now it is high time to awake out of sleep: for now is our salvation nearer than when we believed. The night is far spent, the day is at hand: let us, who are of the day, be sober. Put on for an helmet, the hope of salvation. For God has not appointed us to wrath, but to obtain salvation by our Lord Jesus Christ.

From childhood we have known the holy scriptures, which are able to make us wise unto salvation through faith which is in Christ Jesus. For all scripture is given by inspiration of God, and is profitable for doctrine, for reproof, for correction, for instruction in righteousness: that we may be perfect, thoroughly furnished unto all good works.

We will rejoice in Your salvation, and in the name of our God we will set up our banners: the Lord will fulfill all our petitions.

Now know the Lord saves His anointed; He will hear them from His holy heaven with the saving strength of His right hand.

Some trust in chariots, and some in horses: but we will remember the name of the Lord our God. They are brought down and fallen: but we are risen, and stand upright.

Show us Your ways, O Lord; teach us Your paths. Lead us in Your truth, and teach us: for You are the God of our salvation; we look to you all the time. The Lord is our light and our salvation; whom shall we fear? The Lord is the strength of our life; of whom shall we be afraid?

The salvation of the righteous is of the Lord: He is their strength in the time of trouble. And the Lord shall help them, and deliver them: He shall deliver them from the wicked, and save them, because they trust in Him.

Therefore we pray: "Make haste to help me, O Lord my salvation."

Truly our souls wait upon God: from Him comes our salvation. He only is our rock and our salvation; He is our defense; we shall not be moved. In God is our salvation and our glory: the rock of our strength, and our refuge, is in God. We ought to trust in Him at all times.

We call on the Lord, who is worthy to be praised: so we will be saved from our enemies. When the waves of death pound us on every side, the floods of ungodly men make us afraid, the sorrows of hell surround us, we in our distress called upon the Lord, and cried to our God: and He did hear our voice, and our cry did enter into His ears.

Then the earth shook and trembled; the foundations of heaven moved and shook, because He was filled with anger. There went up a smoke out of His nostrils, and fire out of His mouth devoured: coals were kindled by it. He bowed the heavens also and came down; and darkness was under His feet. And He rode upon a cherub, and did fly: and He was seen upon the wings of the wind. And He made darkness pavilions round about him, dark waters, and thick clouds of the skies. A brightness went before Him and kindled coals of fire.

We shall not need to fight in this battle: we set ourselves, we stand still, and see the salvation of the Lord. We fear not, nor are we dismayed; for the Lord is with us..

So shall they fear the name of the Lord from the west, and His glory from the rising of the sun. When the enemy shall come in like a flood, the Spirit of the Lord shall lift up a standard against him. He will keep us from the hands of the wicked; He will preserve us from violent men, who have purposed to overthrow our goings.

The Lord, the strength of my salvation, has covered my head in the day of battle. The Lord will dash the enemy in pieces. And in the greatness of His excellency He will overthrow them that rose up against us: He will send forth His wrath, which will consume them as stubble.

And we will hear a loud voice saying in heaven, "Now is come salvation, and strength, and the kingdom of Your God, and the power of His Christ: for the accuser is cast down, which accused them before our God day and night. We have overcome him by the blood of the Lamb.

REFERENCES:

Ps. 140:7

Isa. 61:10

Acts 4:12

Rom. 10:9

Rom. 13:11–12

1 Thess. 5:5

2 Tim. 3:15–17

Ps. 20:5–8

Ps. 25:4–5

Ps. 27:1

Ps. 37:39–40

Ps. 38:22

Ps. 62:1–2, 7

2 Sam. 22:2–13

2 Chron. 20:17

Isa. 59:17–19

Ps. 140:4–7

Exod. 15:6–7

Rev. 12:10–11

Ephesians 6:17

Receive the
sword
of the Spirit,
which is the
word of God.

Legionary (left) in combat with Dacian enemy,
from a monument at Adamklissi, Romania.

The Sword of the Spirit

In Paul's inventory of equipment for the Christian soldier only one offensive weapon is listed: the sword. The sword he refers to is the *gladius*—the Roman legionary's sword—with which most of the Roman empire was won. With a short tonguelike blade, the *gladius* was designed more for thrusting than swinging. Soldiers got close to their enemies under the protection of their shields, then used their swords to deadly effect. The blade of the sword was made of iron from Spain and known for its balance. When not in use, it was kept in a decorated wooden sheath to prevent rusting. Interestingly, Paul reminds the reader that the sword he refers to is the Spirit's. It will be wielded by His strength and skill in the hand of one who knows the Word, for the Scriptures tell us the role of the Spirit is to speak what He hears concerning the Word of God.

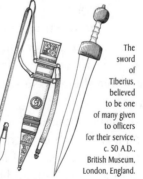

The sword of Tiberius, believed to be one of many given to officers for their service, c. 50 A.D., British Museum, London, England.

Be merciful unto us, O God, be merciful unto us: for our souls trust in You: yes, in the shadow of Your wings do we make our refuge, until these calamities pass by.

The Lord is near to all them that call upon Him, to all that call upon Him in truth. He will fulfill the desire of them that fear Him: He also will hear their cry, and will save them. The Lord preserves all them that love Him: but all the wicked will He destroy.

Thus, we cry to God most high; to God who performs all things for us. He shall send from heaven and save us from the reproach of him that would swallow us up. God shall send forth His mercy and His truth. The salvation of the righteous is of the Lord: He is their strength in the time of trouble. The Lord shall help them and deliver them: He shall deliver them from the wicked, and save them because they trust in Him.

Plead our cause, O Lord, with them that strive with us: fight against them that fight against us. Take hold of shield and buckler, and stand up for our help. Draw out also the spear, and stop the way against them that persecute us: say to our souls, "I am your salvation." Let them be confounded and put to shame that seek after our souls: let them be turned back and brought to confusion that devise our hurt. For our souls are among lions: and we lie even among them that are set on fire, even the sons of men, whose teeth are spears and arrows, and their tongue a sharp sword. They have prepared a net for our steps; our souls are bowed down. Every day they wrest our words: all their thoughts are against us for evil. They gather themselves together, they hide themselves, they mark our steps, they wait for our souls. The wicked have drawn out the sword, and have bent their bow, to cast down the poor and needy, and to slay such as be of upright conversation.

The wicked have waited for us to destroy us: but we will consider Your testimonies, Lord. We will give no thought to how or what we shall speak: for it shall be given us in that same hour what we shall speak. For it is not we that speak, but the Spirit. In God we will praise His word, in God we will put our trust; we will not fear what flesh can do to us.

Their sword shall enter into their own heart, and their bows shall be broken. Evil shall slay the wicked: and they that hate the righteous shall be desolate. A little that righteous men have is better than the riches of many wicked. For the arms of the wicked shall be broken: but the Lord upholds the righteous.

Heaven opened, and behold a white horse; and He that sat upon him was called Faithful and True, and in righteousness He does judge and make war. His eyes were as a flame of fire, and His countenance was as the sun shining in full strength, and on His head were many crowns; and He had a name written, that no man knew, but He himself. And He was clothed with a vesture dipped in blood: and His name is called The Word of God. And the armies which were in heaven followed Him upon white horses, clothed in fine linen, white and clean.

And out of His mouth goes a sharp sword, that with it He should smite the nations: and He shall rule them with a rod of iron: and He treads the wine-press of the fierceness and wrath of Almighty God. There broke He the arrows of the bow, the shield, and the sword. He says, "I whet my glittering sword, and mine hand takes hold on judgment; I will render vengeance to mine enemies, and will reward them that hate Me. I will make mine arrows drunk with blood, and my sword shall devour flesh; and that with the blood of the slain and of the captives, form the beginning of revenge upon the enemy."

Rejoice, for He will avenge the blood of His servants and will render vengeance to His adversaries, and will be merciful unto His land, and to His people. Let the high praises of God be in our mouth, and a two-edged sword in our hand to execute vengeance upon the heathen, and punishments upon the wicked.

Oh, let the wickedness of the wicked come to an end; but establish the just. Our defense is of God, which saves the upright in heart. God judges the righteous, and God is angry with the wicked every day. If they do not repent and change their ways God will whet His sword; He has bent His bow, and made it ready. He has prepared for the wicked the instruments of death; He ordains His arrows against the persecutors.

Therefore will we hew them by the prophets; we will slay them by the words of God's mouth: and His judgments are as the light that goes forth. We will pursue our enemies and destroy them; and we will not turn again until we have consumed them. And we have consumed them, and wounded them, that they could not arise: yes, they are fallen under our feet.

You have also given us the necks of our enemies, that we might destroy them that hate us. They looked, but there was none to save; even to the Lord, but He will answer them not.

Then will we beat them as small as the dust of the earth, we will stamp them as the mire of the street, and will spread them abroad. Let them be as chaff before the wind: and let the angel of the Lord chase them. Let their way be dark and slippery: and let the angel of the Lord persecute them. So it shall be at the end of the world; the angels shall come forth, and sever the wicked from among the just, and shall cast them into the furnace of fire: there shall be wailing and gnashing of teeth.

So do not fret because of evildoers, neither should we be envious against the workers of iniquity. For they shall soon be cut down like the grass, and wither as the green herb. Trust in the Lord, and do good, so that you will dwell in the land, and truly you will be fed. Delight yourself also in the Lord and He shall give you the desires of your heart. This was written unto you, fathers, because you have known Him that is from the beginning. This is written to you, young men, because you are strong, and the word of God abides in you, and you have overcome the wicked one.

Happy will we be, people saved by the Lord, the shield of our help, and who is the sword of excellency! And our enemies shall be found liars unto Him; and He shall tread upon their high places. He will give them that are wicked to the sword.

Unless Your law had been our delight, we would then have perished. I will never forget Your precepts: for with them You have brought me to life. We are Yours, for I have sought Your precepts. Teach us to do Your will; for You are our God: Your Spirit is good; lead us into the land of uprightness. Let our cry come near before You, O Lord: give us understanding according to Your word. Let our supplication come before You: deliver us according to Your word. Teach us, O Lord, the way of Your statutes; and we shall keep it unto the end. Give us understanding, and we shall keep Your law; yes, we shall observe it with our whole heart. Make us to go in the path of Your commandments; for therein do we delight.

Therefore create in us a clean heart, O God; and renew a right spirit within us. Do not cast us away from Your presence; and take not Your Holy Spirit from us. Restore unto us the joy of Your salvation; and uphold us with Your free spirit.

For You will give us a new heart, and a new spirit will You put within us: and You will take away the stony heart out of our flesh, and You will give us an heart of flesh. And You will put Your Spirit within us, and cause us to walk in Your statutes, and we shall keep Your judgments, and do them. You will pour out Your Spirit to us. You will make known Your words unto us.

Likewise the Spirit also helps our infirmities: for we know not what we should pray for as we should: but the Spirit Himself makes intercession for us with groanings which cannot be uttered.

We will be renewed in the spirit of our mind; for the word of God is quick, and powerful, and sharper than any two-edged sword, piercing even to the dividing asunder of soul and spirit, and of the joints and marrow, and is a discerner of the thoughts and intents of the heart. Neither is there any creature that is not manifest in His sight: but all things are naked and opened unto the eyes of Him with whom we have to do. We therefore will not be condemned if we are in Christ Jesus, and walk not after the flesh, but after the Spirit. For the law of the Spirit of life in Christ Jesus has made us free from the law of sin and death. For what the law could not do, in that it was weak through the flesh, God sending His own Son in the likeness of sinful flesh, and for sin, condemned sin in the flesh: that the righteousness of the law might be fulfilled in us, who walk not after the flesh, but after the Spirit. For they that are after the flesh do mind the things of the flesh; but they that are after the Spirit the things of the Spirit. For to be ruled in your minds by the flesh is death; but to be ruled in your minds by the Spirit is life and peace. Because the mind governed by the flesh is at odds with God: for it is not subject to the law of God, neither indeed can be. So then they that are in the flesh cannot please God. But we are not in the flesh but in the Spirit, if so be that the Spirit of God dwell in us. Now if any man have not the Spirit of Christ, he is none of

His. And if Christ be in you, the body is dead because of sin; but the Spirit is life because of righteousness. But if the Spirit of Him that raised up Jesus from the dead dwell in us, He that raised up Christ from the dead shall also bring to life our mortal bodies by His Spirit that dwells in us. Therefore, we are in debt, not to the flesh, to live after the flesh. For if we live after the flesh, we shall die: but if we through the Spirit do put to death the deeds of the body, we shall live. For as many as are led by the Spirit of God, they are the sons of God. For we have not received the spirit of bondage again to fear; but we have received the Spirit of adoption, where-by we cry, Abba, Father.

The Spirit Himself bears witness with our spirit, that we are the children of God: Therefore, if we continue in Your word, then we are Your disciples indeed; by the word of truth, by the power of God, by the armor of righteousness on the right hand and on the left.

REFERENCES:

Ps. 57:1
Ps. 145:18–20
Ps. 57:2–3
Ps. 37:39–40
Ps. 35:1–4
Ps. 57:4, 6
Ps. 56:5–6
Ps. 37:14
Ps. 119:95
Mark 13:11
Ps. 56:4
Ps. 37:15
Ps. 34:21
Ps. 37:16–17
Rev. 19:11–15
Ps. 76:3
Deut. 34:41–43
Ps. 149:6–7
Ps. 7: 9–13
Hos. 6:5
Ps. 18: 37–38

2 Sam. 22: 39–43
Ps. 35: 56
Matt. 13:49–50
Ps. 37:1–4
John 2:14
Deut. 33:29
Jer. 25:31
Ps. 119:92–94
Ps. 143:10
Ps. 119:169–70
Ps. 119:33–35
Ps. 51:10–12
Ezek. 37:26–27
Prov. 1:23
Rom. 8:26
Eph. 4:23
Heb. 4:12–13
Rom. 8:1–16
John 8:31
2 Cor. 6:7

PRAY ALWAYS
WITH ALL PRAYER
AND SUPPLICATION
IN THE SPIRIT,
AND WATCH
WITH ALL PERSEVERANCE
AND SUPPLICATION
FOR ALL SAINTS.
FOR I AM PERSUADED,
THAT NEITHER DEATH, NOR LIFE,
NOR ANGELS,
NOR PRINCIPALITIES,
NOR POWERS,
NOR THINGS PRESENT,
NOR THINGS TO COME,
NOR HEIGHT, NOR DEPTH,
NOR ANY OTHER CREATURE,
SHALL BE ABLE TO SEPARATE US
FROM THE LOVE OF GOD,
WHICH IS IN
CHRIST JESUS OUR LORD.

The Christian Armory is based on the apostle Paul's teaching found in verses ten through eighteen of chapter six of his letter to the Ephesians. Related verses throughout the Bible were researched and compiled to form the text of this work.

The King James Version of the Bible was used in compiling verses, and careful attention was paid to preserve the original intent of each passage selected. The text was then updated for today's reader: archaic pronouns changed to the contemporary we, he, you, etc.; outdated or unfamiliar terms replaced with up-to-date equivalents; pronouns referring to the Godhead were capitalized; and quotation marks added to clarify who is being quoted. The result is a paraphrase of the King James Version and no similarity to any other contemporary Bible version is intended.

Connectives such as therefore, for, and, because, etc. were added to make the text read in a flowing manner.

A list of references noted in the same order as each passage appears is provided at the end of each section for further study.